SCANDINAVIA

Marion Sichel

Chelsea House Publishers
New York • New Haven • Philadelphia

© Marion Sichel 1987
First published 1987

Printed in Great Britain

Published in U.S.A. by
Chelsea House Publishers
5014 West Chester Pike
Edgemont, Pa., 19028

Published in the U.K. by
B T Batsford Limited
4 Fitzhardinge Street, London W1H 0AH

Library of Congress Cataloging-in-Publication Data

Sichel, Marion.
  Scandinavia.

  (National costume reference)
  Bibliography: p.
  Includes index.
  Summary: Describes the national costumes of Norway,
Sweden, Finland, Lapland, Denmark, Iceland, and
Greenland, and explores the historical, religious, and social
contexts in which they are appropriately worn.
  1. Costume—Scandinavia—Juvenile literature.
[1. Costume—Scandinavia. 2. Scandinavia—Social life
and customs] I. Title. II. Series.
GT1100.S52 1988   391′.00948   87-14643

ISBN 1-55546-739-3

Caption to jacket illustration

*The man on the left is wearing an
eastern Telemark costume. The Lapp
is in the dress characteristic of the
Nordkalotten district in Sweden. The
small girl in the centre is from
Denmark. The young Swedish lady
wears the costume originating from
Dalarna. At the back is a girl from
Greenland and on the right a girl
from Iceland, both in their
traditional dress*

*This girl from Leksand, Dalarna, is
wearing a boldly striped apron over a
skirt, with a small laced yoke held up
with braces. Her white bonnet is
edged with lace*

CONTENTS

In winter a muffler made of many squirrels' tails is wound twice around the neck for protection against the cold. The coat is held in place with a woollen girdle up to five metres long, tied around the waist and crossed over the chest. The warm mittens are made from the hide of bears or wolves

PREFACE

An embroidered bodice from Gudrandsdal, Sweden

One of the most important features of a volume of this kind is the large number of illustrations, and these have been chosen from many examples of the folk costumes of the past.

Because of the great variety of costumes, not only in various districts, but also in individual styles, there may be several costumes depicting one area or district.

With the revival of the old crafts and traditions in the twentieth century, the interest in local costumes was stimulated.

Where there were no originals available, replicas of these costumes were made and worn for festivals and on other special occasions.

Many of the inherited skills and traditional designs have been adapted throughout Scandinavia for use in their hand embroidery and knitted sweaters which continue to be in great demand abroad.

My thanks go to the staffs of the various embassies whose assistance was most helpful. Also my grateful thanks to Thelma Nye of Batsford for her great help and encouragement as always.

Norwegian Lapp girl wearing a bonnet decorated with braid and a kolte in royal blue decorated with a coloured embroidered band. She is holding a bundle of dried grass

4

INTRODUCTION

A dress from Valdres. The bodice fastens at the top. The purse hangs from her belt, an essential part of the festival dress of Norway

Scandinavia consists of Norway, Sweden, Denmark, Finland and Iceland, all linked by historical and geographical ties. Greenland is officially a constituent part of Denmark, although now self-governing. In both social and traditional terms these countries have many characteristics in common.

Historically the five Nordic countries were first united in 1397; a union which lasted until the secession of Sweden in 1523. Although there is no such country as Lapland, the most northerly parts of Norway, namely Finmark, and the arctic and sub-areas of northern Sweden and Finland, are inhabited by the Lapps, an indiginous minority who have their own language and culture.

Folk costume is the distinctive traditional dress worn in different regions, whether geographical or social. In 1874 William Morris began an Arts and Crafts revival in Britain that encouraged other similar revivals in Scandinavia, and these included a new interest in the folk dress once worn everyday by country people, and was similar throughout Europe in the Middle Ages, usually being made of homespun cloth.

Throughout Scandinavia many skilled handicrafts are practised, such as leatherwork, silverwork, weaving, knitting and embroidery.

The Lapps' dress is one of the most ancient of the costumes worn in western Europe, due to its total suitability to their way of life.

The Norwegian folk dress is said to be the most elegant. A great deal of time is spent on the embroidered decorations with intricate designs worked in whitework, blackwork and cross stitch as well as the characteristic *rosesaum* or rosework.

There are also many costumes in Sweden, each with its own history, and any newcomer to a community was required to adopt the costume of that particular society. During their civil war this was a method of recognising friend from foe.

Having been a province of Sweden in the past, the Finnish

costumes bear a resemblance to the Swedish styles, although in the eastern parts, such as in Karelia, the Russian trends can be seen. Many of the basic styles in these remote regions date back to the Middle Ages.

Icelandic costume is similar throughout the country due to the few regional differences, and also the small population that is centred in just one small area.

A girl on skis at the beginning of the twentieth century, wearing a long plain pleated skirt, a full sleeved white blouse and a red sleeveless waistcoat with a dark embroidered plastron

NORWAY

Typical Norwegian costume now mainly worn at dance festivals

Norway, in northern Europe, is on the western side of the Scandinavian peninsula and forms a strip of irregular and mountainous coastland some 3,200 km long facing the North Sea and Atlantic and Arctic Oceans. On the south it is bounded by the Skagerrak – the water which separates it from Denmark, and on the east by Russia, Finland and Sweden. The majority of the country, especially in the north, consists of mountainous plateaux with immense glaciers and innumerable rivers and lakes. It is only towards the south that there is any low-lying land, a very small percentage of which can be cultivated or used for grazing animals. The wealth of the country lies in its forests and fisheries as well as in shipping. The climate inland can be intensely cold, whereas those districts on the west coast benefit from the warm drift of the Gulf Stream.

The Norwegians are a democratic people, titles and nobility having been abolished in 1821. They have two paralled classes: the well educated, living mainly in the urban districts, and the country people or *bönder* of the rural areas who take great pride in wearing local dress and continue to keep their folk costume alive today.

With so many small isolated communities, Norway is a country with a continuing tradition of folk costume which has been stimulated by a revival of interest in local crafts and traditions. Whilst once an individual style might belong to a small area such as a village, a particular trade or even to a church group, a much more general style applies today, the men's based on the Telemark costume and the women's on that of the popular dress from Hardanger. There are, however, still clear distinctive styles of dress between east and west, and those of the interior are freer in form and colour schemes than those in coastal areas which tend to be basically black and white.

In medieval times both men and women wore much the same style of dress, differing only in length and colour. The women's dress was calf length, usually black or red, although sometimes made of a natural coloured wool. Different coloured edgings

A warm cap and reindeer hide shoes are worn by this young Norwegian from the north

7

denoted the different areas from which the wearers came. The men had long smock-like garments with long sleeves and ankle length trousers. The 'smock' usually had a belt from which hung such things as keys, sheathed knives and an array of tools, as there were no pockets in those days.

A short cape with a hood attached was worn in inclement weather, much the same as in the rest of Europe at that time. For warmth, cloth stockings reaching the knees or slightly higher, were worn with soft heelless shoes, but if, as was sometimes seen, the stockings were made of leather, shoes were unnecessary.

The coarse white kirtle or blouse was later worn beneath a jacket, eventually becoming a chemise for women, and an undershirt for men. When made of delicate and expensive linen, these garments were embroidered on the sleeves and front and were no longer regarded as underwear, becoming a blouse or shirt.

Medieval style costumes remained in vogue until the eighteenth century with little change, and even in the early nineteenth century the elderly could still be seen wearing the older styles. Renaissance modes, however, dominated fashion, the main influence coming from Spain.

Although popular in eastern Norway, the fjord and mountain districts did not follow the fashions, but towards the end of the eighteenth century a more picturesque and practical attire became the national style. This consists of close fitting breeches with knee buckles, a red or white flared jacket and several underjackets in diverse colours and ornamentation.

Silver and pewter buttons in great profusion, replaced the clasps although not all were functional, the only jacket fastening being on the one worn innermost. By leaving the overjackets open, the decorative braids and embroidery on the borders and seams were visible.

Towards the middle of the nineteenth century the mountain and fjord districts developed their own style of dress. The hip length jackets were replaced by much shorter ones with a high standing collar, and in several districts long trousers, narrow at the base, had placket openings with buttons at the lower edges.

The low necked, sleeveless bodice with a colourful *plastron* and the dark, usually blue or black skirt, were joined at the waist with a belt. Aprons, not seen much before the Renaissance, were worn in dark colours for special occasions. In winter a black jacket was also worn.

A girl from Telemark wearing a long full skirt with a wide woven belt, and a short long-sleeved jacket

The man from Telemark is in a short jacket with a high standing collar, reminiscent of the Empire period, and a broad-brimmed hat is being carried

This costume, the foundation of later styles, originated in the seventeenth century and was little altered except for variations to differentiate the regions.

On 17 May of each year Constitution Day is celebrated throughout Norway, the most extensive celebrations being held in the capital city, Oslo, where hundreds of young people parade waving flags. The school children wear their traditional scarlet peaked caps with tassels and scarlet waistcoats decorated with the emblems of their particular schools. The boys carry walking sticks trimmed with scarlet ribbons and the girls carry scarlet unbrellas. The students wear their black caps, each with a long heavy tassel which should rest on their right shoulder.

On Midsummer Eve there is countrywide celebration with bonfires and processions of children in national costume.

The most characteristic of Norwegian embroidery is *rosesaum* or rosework. This is a type of wool embroidery worked in the rococo style. The design and colour varies from district to district but it is found on any type of material from velvet to canvas, although its use on woollen fabrics is the most common. The most representative designs are petal and tear-drop shapes worked in satin stitch.

Western Norway, however, is renowned for white embroidery, Hardanger work being the most widely known. This is used extensively to decorate the bodice and is shown to good effect on white aprons worn over dark skirts.

Around the mid-nineteenth century, mass market fashions penetrated rural areas, thus ending much of the home weaving and hand embroidery. However, many of the older traditional costumes had been so well made that they became heirlooms and are handed down through generations.

The region of Telemark has at least six districts which vary from north to south and east to west, as well as in the mountainous and valley areas. Those nearer the western coastal cities adopted new trends the fastest and these were then passed to the valleys. The poorer and often most isolated districts were the last to accept any new innovations.

In Telemark the man's dress consists of a white jacket with black embroidery over a black waistcoat, and black knee breeches. The standing collar of the white shirt is fastened by two silver filigree buttons. Buttons and lacing rings or *maler* decorate either side of the jacket opening and the lapels and high collar are richly embroidered. Knitted white stockings and black leather shoes with silver buckles complete the costume.

9

The Empire style dress was very popular with the women, the high waisted skirt hanging from a narrow yoke or braces-like straps. Skirts were worn long and full in both Telemark and Hallingdal, just to the north, and these had wide colourful belts of woven fabrics. The skirts are generally black or dark blue with black, dark green or red bodices. Short red or blue long-sleeved jackets could also be worn. The people of Hallingdal adapted this dress to bring it up to date by the use of brightly coloured trimmings and accessories, including a complicated headdress design with coloured fringes.

An older style from Hallingdal consists of a long dark red skirt with coloured bands at the hem, over which was worn a full length apron. The bodice, matching the skirt, has wide trimmings in the front which was open to reveal the heavy silver jewellery. The black cap, bound with coloured ribbon, is framed with frilled lacing. The men's costume consists of light homespun jackets worn with yellow breeches embroidered down the sides, and red embroidered caps.

On the east side of Telemark the bodice is waist length, richly embroidered and edged with contrasting bands of colour. Prominence is given to the lacing rings or *maler* which give added decoration. The collar and cuffs of blouses are covered with cross stitch or *glit* as well as *rosesaum* embroidery.

Young girls wear simple headbands, but a more distinctive style is a flat shape fastened towards the back of the head and covered with a silk kerchief which can be draped and arranged in a wide variety of ways.

South west of Telemark lies Setesdal, a small isolated mountainous district with a unique costume which has survived intact to this day. A white blouse with a rounded collar is worn beneath the high waisted skirt which is pleated in such a way as to give the appearance of wide trousers, reaching just below knee length.

For everyday wear the skirt is of white wool with three black stripes around the hem. It is gathered onto a narrow yoke, held up by short embroidered shoulder straps and a wide black leather belt. For festive occasions the dress, of the same shape but shorter, is black with red or green bands stiffened with hoops at the hem to give the effect of a divided skirt. The dark bodice, edged with green, is fastened with silver chains. It is worn over the top of the everyday garment, the blouse of which can be seen beneath it at the neck and wrists and below the very short bolero. The belt would be embroidered with cross stitch

A child in Hallingdal costume

Hallingdal costume: the plaid apron has a leather belt at the waist, and the ever-popular brooch is worn on the blouse. This outfit is mainly for everyday wear

Knitted stocking cap from Setesdal

A woman in a Telemark dress without a jacket, the embroidery, a rosesaum *design is seen on the dark skirt. A large brooch is worn on the embroidered blouse and the reticule hangs from the belt*

to match that on the straps of the bodice. Long-sleeved jackets are worn in winter. A red and black kerchief is worn to cover the head or, for warmth, a fringed red woollen cap and a striped shawl or *tjeld* is worn around the shoulders.

A distinctive feature of this Setesdal costume is that brides would wear yet a third skirt, the one over the other, the third being the shortest, in red with a silver band at the hem. The belt would usually be of silver with streamers hanging from it. Setesdal is renowned for its silverwork of traditional design and is much worn locally.

Men's costume consists of high-bibbed trousers, reaching to the armpits, with short jackets allowing the embroidery and often filigree buttons, which decorate the bibs, to be seen. The seats of the trousers are reinforced with large decorative patches. A festive style consists of long black trousers reaching from the shoulders to the ankles, held up by short leather braces with metal clasps. The trousers have low cut sides, and the bib is embroidered in scarlet with green trimmings. Very short sleeveless jackets display the full sleeved white shirts with a lace edged collar beneath. Broad brimmed black hats complete the outfits. This style of costume was also worn by young boys.

Vest-Agder, the southernmost district of Norway, was a flourishing trading area from ancient times. As much trade was with the Netherlands they brought back many of the Dutch ideas, including dress. The women's costume consists of a skirt slightly longer and lower waisted than that of the Setesdal area. It is made of black wool with three coloured bands at the hemline, two red with a green strip in between, with braces buttoned on at the waist. The waistband is cut to a peak at the centre back. The bodice, shaped to the figure of the wearer, has a lowish neckline and twelve silver lacing rings or *maler* on either side of the opening. Although tightly laced at the bottom, it becomes looser and may even be unlaced at the top. Silver brooches or clasps are pinned to the white blouse and also to the bodice on either side of the lacing. Silver buckles are worn on the shoes. In winter long sleeved jackets with cuffs are worn, similar in cut to the bodices except that instead of lacing, hooks are used.

The Hardanger costume is one of the best known of Norway's folk dress, and has altered very little since the early nineteenth century except that the waistline has been lowered, and the skirts, originally dark blue, are now black and the bodice generally red, green or brown with contrasting borders.

The embroidery on the *plastron* and belt is mainly beadwork, which has been substituted for the older type of decoration with wool.

The original Hardanger dress consists of a tightly gathered blue woollen skirt and a red bodice with blue or brown borders. Typical of the costume is the white blouse and apron with white Hardanger openwork embroidery. This is a white border in geometric shapes with stepped edges, giving a diagonal effect. The network of threads is darned into bars and the edges of the designs buttonholed. One or more brooches complete the costume.

There are two styles of headdress, both white. One consists of a finely pleated kerchief shaped like a bonnet to frame the face, with the point standing out stiffly at the back. The other style is wing shaped, covered by a large unpleated kerchief which falls loosely at the back.

Children and young girls often wear a square headdress of scarlet velvet or a woollen fabric, edged with black velvet and embroidered with beadwork.

Although a widespread tradition, Hardanger especially is noted for its *crown weddings*, so called because with her festive national dress the bride wears a gold or silver crown, often an heirloom, which is elaborately decorated with garlands and pendants.

A traditional wedding processsion can still be seen in Voss where not only the bride and groom but also most of the guests will be wearing national costume. The type of crown worn in this area is one of the most unusual. It is 'B' shaped, and worn horizontally so that the pendants hang down around the head. These are generally heart shaped with the larger ones on either side, the smaller ones at the back. The top of the crown is covered in beading.

In some areas the headdress is turban shaped covered with silk cloth upon which numerous silver discs tinkle with every movement. As well as all the usual jewellery, the bride may wear a large oval collar which is fastened at the shoulders and is covered with brooches.

Another important accessory to the bridal outfit is the belt, which is a series of metal plates fastened to a cloth base with chain or cloth streamers ornamented with silver, hanging at the front. One or two heavy chains with pendants are worn around the neck, one of which is always a gift from the groom. Rings are also worn, although earrings and bracelets are hardly ever seen.

Young girl from Hardangar with a colourful and decorated band around her head. The narrow yoke of her dress is covered in brooches

Hardanger type costume: white bonnet is pleated and worn with a tightly gathered skirt. The brightly beaded plastron *and belt, both in geometrical designs have replaced the older style embroidery*

A bridegroom's costume from Hallingdal

Little girl from Hallindal with a band around her hair, streamers hanging behind

A costume from Hardanger. The sleeveless bodice is fastened with lacing, the top open to reveal the plastron and highnecked blouse. The apron is embroidered at the hem in Hardanger work and a reticule hangs from the belt at the waist

Outfit from Hardanger The dark coloured bodice is laced with silver, and the headdress resembles that of a nun. The plastron is decorated with a geometrical design and on the blouse is an ornate brooch

Silver sun brooch from Hardanger

Voss bridal headdress that rests across the top of the head with decorations hanging from the side pieces. The apron is decorated in blackwork

All bridal costumes are worn with low heeled black shoes and black stockings. Knee garters, visible beneath the shorter styles of skirt, are woven in bright colours or embroidered and tasseled.

The bridegroom wears black velvet knee breeches and jacket with a scarlet waistcoat edged with green hand stitchery. A silver brooch is used to fasten the collar of the white linen shirt. Knitted white woollen stockings are worn with silver buckled black leather shoes.

Like Hardanger, both Sogn and Voss use geometric designs, and if *rosesaum* embroidery was not used on the dress itself, the purse or reticule which hung from the belt was so embroidered.

Voss, just north of Hardanger, and Fana near Bergen have similar costumes to those worn in Hardanger. The bodice, embroidered with small white beads, is usually red, but the borders could vary in colour. For example in Fana they could be blue with white beading, whilst in Voss, where the bodice is much less deep across the back, has a green velvet border with white beads and silver thread. The *plastron* is beaded or embroidered with complex geometric designs. The lower edge of the skirt also has a wide green velvet band with silver lace at the top. A white apron decorated with drawn thread work is also worn.

The headdress of Fana is high and round with points at the sides, whilst that of Voss consists of a white embroidered triangular kerchief or *skaut* tied over a leather framework to enable it to stand out stiffly behind. Young girls, however, wear a coloured band fastened at the back of the head with a silver clasp, or a small red embroidered bonnet tied on with ribbons. Black stockings and black leather shoes with silver buckles are also worn.

The costumes of the Sogn district, although basically the same as for other areas, differ in the length of the skirt which is shorter and often has a band of coloured fabric appliquéd around the base rather than stripes set in. In Sogn, characteristic appliqué work consists of intricate scrolls and pierced designs on skirts, aprons and on children's clothes. Red, green and blue are the usual colours, red being the most common. Red backgrounds always have blue or green designs, whilst green always have red. Black could have any colour combination appliquéd to it. The white blouses are decorated mainly with whitework and/or blackwork. The line borders are usually worked in Holbein stitch in a lily motif. Cross stitch or

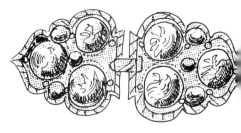

A jacket clasp from Hallingdal

Hardanger bridal costume. Several chains with pendants are worn around the neck, and the tall headdress is also decorated with pendants

A sleeveless jacket as worn in Voss

A Sogn costume with a black skirt embroidered at the base. The plastron *is embroidered and in cool weather a long sleeved jacket can be worn under the bodice, as is seen here*

glit is also common especially on *plastrons*. Brooches are worn in profusion, and chains to lace up bodices and sometimes blouse openings. Neck chains are used to hold pendants.

The bodice, ending just above the waistline, could be laced or worn open with a *plastron*. The edges are faced in a contrasting colour and in cold weather a long-sleeved jacket would be worn beneath.

The skirts, although usually black, could be of dark coloured stripes or a plaid design. The aprons worn on festive occasions are usually dark in a contrasting colour to the skirt, or with contrasting stripes. Several types of belt are in use, such as leather with rectangular silver plates close together, having pendants hanging from the plates, and closed with a silver clasp. A red streamer denotes married status. Canvas belts are studded with brass or silver nail heads, and beaded belts are also worn. A large embroidered purse nearly always hangs from the belt.

There are two types of headdress: a small black brimless bonnet tied under the chin bedecked with ribbons and beading and a white cap distended at the sides and bound with a silk scarf and white ruching to frame the face. In summer young girls wear around the head a *bara* which is a band of fabric about 12 cm wide. In winter a grey woollen cap is worn.

There are many distinctive knitted designs special to certain areas, and Fana has a jacket knitted in two colours with a geometric eight-petal rose design across the top of the sleeves, with the centre part having alternate rows of dots and small geometric designs.

In the Nordfjord area the costume of the valley consists of a skirt and jacket as well as an apron, all of black material. The flower embroidered jacket has velvet edging at the neck, and the apron has black or white flowered embroidery. A long-sleeved bodice could be worn in place of the jacket, and this is usually blue with green sleeves or vice versa. For special occasions a silk neckerchief is worn tucked in the front.

The headwear is so complicated that it requires help with the arrangement. A headband is first put on so that the hat can be pinned in such a way that it is perched on the back of the head, and over this is placed a black silk kerchief with a coloured border.

Sunnöre, on the west coast, has a dark dress, different from Other areas on the west. The bodice neckline is higher and without a *plastron*, although the embroidered neckline of the blouse is visible. The shoulder extensions and the cuffs of the blouse are also embroidered, all in white.

The bodice, skirt and apron, all black, are embroidered in multi-coloured designs. From the belt would hang an embroidered purse. The headdress consists of either a small black velvet bonnet, tied beneath the chin, or a white scarf hanging over the shoulders at the back.

In the valley of Romsdal the bodice is red with *rosesaum* embroidery and a dark coloured skirt with similar embroidery around the hem, but on a smaller scale. The blouses and aprons are white. The dark coloured cap is in a style similar to the Dutch, with flaps on either side.

The most common costume from Röros, in the east, is a long-sleeved dark coloured dress with light coloured trimmings. The full sleeves are gathered at the wrists and the pleated skirt often has the hem faced in a contrasting colour. Silk shawls in various colours are an important feature and are often handed down as heirlooms.

The married woman from Hardanger is wearing a bonnet and a sun brooch on her blouse

The headwear, a small silk cap tied beneath the chin, is brown with a red or pink band, specially embroidered for festive occasions for young girls, whilst unmarried women wear black caps with white star designs in glass beads. Married women's caps are entirely black, even to the ribbon bands.

Selbu, further north-east, near Tröndlag, is noted for its mittens, the palms of which have a small all-over design, whilst on the back are reindeer figures or rose designs. The cuffs could be in contrasting colour with lace stitch designs.

The costumes from Tröndlag, more typical of the east Norwegian costumes, have a white brocade bodice with a peplum, closed at the waist with clasps. Dark skirts and contrasting brocade aprons are worn. White blouses and white drawn-thread work headcloths complete these costumes which have recently been revived from an earlier design.

Over the years the costumes have become simpler in eastern Norway. The *plastron* is often omitted, and lacing, although retained, has concealed strings threaded through sewn eyelets on the inside of the bodice opening. The bright borders around the openings are replaced by bright large-scale overall embroidery or with an overall plaid material.

The valley of Gudbrandsdal, which was the most prosperous area of Norway, being the main route from Oslo to the north, developed a very rich and ornate costume for festive wear. A red or pink bodice of silk or wool is decorated with bold flower

The Gudbrandsdal costume consists of a white long sleeved blouse worn over a dark skirt with attached sleeveless bodice open at the waist and with a bold woven flowered design

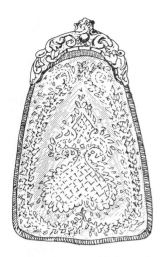

Embroidered purse with brass frame from Sunnmöre

The man from north Tröndelag is wearing moccasins and long stockings. The knee bands end in tassels

designs. It is fastened at the bottom with a *plastron*, the top being left unfastened to give a 'V' effect. A white embroidered blouse with a small frill at neck is worn with a dark full-pleated skirt in elaborate check, striped or embroidered material, with a matching dark apron with coloured embroidery. A gold brocade cap completes the outfit.

For everyday a striped skirt is worn with a red bodice and, for warmth, a short dark jacket. A starched white kerchief is worn over the head.

Flower motifs and vertical stripes are common. Tatting and fringing on blouses and kerchiefs is also popular.

Their shoes are of leather, without heels. In winter laced half-boots are worn.

The men wear breeches and stockings in one piece with waistcoat or jacket to match, all made from homespun wool. For special occasions the style is similar but with seams covered in a different coloured material. They are distinguished from other regions by their distinctive red caps.

Men's dress, worn in the north and east of this area, was seldom seen in the fjord or mountainous districts. It consists of breeches tight to the knees, a brightly coloured waistcoat, and a long tailcoat which has large flap pockets. *Krotasaum*, scrollwork embroidery, is used on men's coats and waistcoats and is typical of the embroidery of this district.

Further east and slightly south in the Hedmark and Österdal districts, plaids are popular, blue being a favourite colour. In Hedmark, in the nineteenth century, a blue jacketed dress with a pleated or gathered skirt, and a close fitting narrow sleeved jacket with a short peplum was worn with a leather belt, but for special occasions the belt was of silver. With this outfit, common throughout Norway in this period, the people of Hedmark wore a small greenish-yellow silk cap and a yellow neckerchief.

Nowadays the blue skirt is embroidered in vertical rows of motifs, the rows about 25 cm apart. The red, yellow and green *rosesaum* embroidered bodice has a red border around the peplum, and the low neckline reveals a white blouse. A blue bonnet with flaps in the Dutch style is embroidered. Men's costume follows the style of Gudbrandsdal, previously described.

Silver played an important role in the life of the country people but because it was mined in the mountains it had become connected with the supernatural mountain folk – the trolls –

giving rise to a great deal of superstition. Jewellery was, however, much treasured and any new piece was always worn first to church as a form of consecration. Charms, handed down from generation to generation, were thought to have magical powers and were used to exorcise any evil spirits.

Many country people wore brass jewellery, but with the arrival of the Renaissance and the subsequent popularity of silver filigree work, brass was relegated to everyday wear, brass buttons and shoe buckles remaining popular.

On the west coast dress was designed to exhibit the jewellery. Silver chains were used to tie the bodices and large brooches were worn in abundance; even everyday clothes were adorned with silver lacing, eyelets, brooches and neckpins.

Although men's attire was not so elaborate, there was, however, still a vast amount of silver in evidence, such as numerous buttons on the waistcoats, and at the knees of the breeches.

Belt buckles were often elaborate but shoe and knee buckles were relatively simple. Belts were strung with ornamental silver plates, and silver knives and sheaths were hung from these belts in the eighteenth century, whilst in the nineteenth century watch chains and fobs became more fashionable.

Pendants are one of the oldest type of peasant jewellery dating back to Viking times. The medallion type of gold pendant, worn as a charm, had runic inscription designs from old Roman coins. The early brooches, about 20 cm long had highly stylised animals and other shapes inscribed and were generally made of silver, decorated with gilt and garnet stones.

With the popular metal lacings, metal eyelets or *maler* were essential. These were at first absolutely plain, but gradually became so ornate that they began to look like buttons with a hole to one side, and finally even the holes were dispensed with when lacings were no longer used. However the *maler* continued in use, more as ornamentation, and with the hooks and eyes attached, used as clasps, sometimes as many as four linked together on either side of an opening. *Maler*, were in fact, versatile pieces of jewellery, being used not only as lacing rings and clasps, but also as belt plates and bridal decoration on the headdresses and collars. As decoration they were more practical than buttons with shanks, as the *maler* lay flat against any material.

The short, open jacket has another type of chain fastener. This chain consists of two clasps or bars fastened either side of

Hallingdal bridegroom with knitted stockings in a geometrical design

18

The white blouse closes high with a large round brooch. The white apron has a border of typical Hardanger work

an opening, sometimes with a central plate. These and the clasps could vary greatly in both shape and design, and there could be several pendants suspended from it.

The most important piece of jewellery was the breast pin, worn in varying numbers by almost everyone throughout Norway. They also varied in shape and size. For instance in the Österdal and Gudbrandsdal districts as well as the north-west coastline, breastpins were usually small and heart-shaped, whereas in the western districts they were more elaborate with hanging pendants.

Small plain pins were generally worn by men at the shirt openings, whilst women wore two or three such pins for everyday wear. For festive occasions larger and more ornate ones were worn in profusion, especially on bridal wear.

Among the many variations one of the oldest types of pins, known as shield pins because they were in the shape of round shields, very often had a round hole in the centre, and a single prong.

A *bursölje* similar to a shield pin, but larger, was worn as a belt buckle. This had six projections, placed in a circle, with sometimes smaller ones in between, the centre one often edged with twisted wire. Shoe and knee buckles were of a much simpler design. They were usually rectangular or oval, with one prong. Knee buckles were smaller versions of those used on shoes. Buttons replaced brooches and buckles when buttoned frock coats and waistcoats became fashionable. Buttons could also be joined together and used as collar and cuff links.

The small population which inhabited the islands off the Norweigan coast developed their own styles which were more appropriate to their needs as fishermen.

Until around 1845, men wore a medieval style jerkin which was replaced by a waistcoat open down the front. Over this they wore a straight hip-length black jacket, lined in green, with a double row of buttons. The calf-length trousers, narrow at the base but fuller at the waist, were worn without belt or braces, being held up by tucking them in over a large pad which encircled the lower edge of the waistcoat. Gradually short jackets and long trousers without a bib front, but with a flap front closing with large silver buttons, became the fashion. The collars became flatter and the shirts longer.

The Island costumes were not as brightly coloured as the others, the jacket, skirt and apron all being dark, the only white being the blouse, a neckerchief and headdress. The bodice beneath the jacket, however, was a bright colour with a beaded or embroidered plastron, silver lacing, brooches and a belt. Underneath the dark finely pleated skirt there could be several more layers of skirts, all brighter than the top one.

The headdress is made of several parts: first a twisted linen roll is placed around the head with a triangular shaped kerchief rolled to frame the face. For daily wear a black cap was worn on top and for festive occasions a white kerchief.

The child is wearing a warm leather cap, a tunic and reindeer hide shoes with knitted stockings, not unlike the attire worn by Lapp children

A man's costume from northern Norway as worn at the beginning of the twentieth century. He is wearing knitted socks over the breeches, a very ornate waistcoat and a tall hat

A costume from Sunnfjord

Worn by a woman from Voss, the bodice is edged with beads and silver lace, and intricate geometric designs are seen on the plastron. The white apron has a whitework design at the base

A woman from north Tröndelag dressed similarly to a Lapp

20

SWEDEN

The woman from Dalarna is in a dress consisting of an embroidered bodice with white sleeves, a dark skirt, an apron, an embroidered cap, and a flat bag attached to the belt around her waist

The girl from Insjon is wearing a coif type headwear and the sleeveless bodice is fastened with lacing

Sweden occupies the largest part of the Scandinavian peninsula. It is separated from Norway on the west by the Kjölen mountains and is bounded by Finland in the north east with the Gulf of Bothnia, and the Baltic Sea lying to the west.

Almost every village and province has its own particular type of dress and these have been carefully perpetuated by a proclamation in 1630 issued to the clergy by Gustavus Adolphus the Great 'to make a note of the dresses, and customs of the people.'.

These national dresses have been influenced by development and frequent changes in style, but with varying results in different parts of the country.

Women's dresses have retained most faithfully their original style, whilst the men have been more easily influenced by the changing fashions.

Knitting, lace making and embroidery play a prominent part in the richly coloured dresses and a girl's marriageability was once judged by the amount and quality of her handiwork. Lace making and linen embroidery still follow the early traditional technique and patterns particularly in the Dalarna and Scania regions.

Typical are white long sleeved blouses, worn by the women, which are gathered at the wrists. They have turned-down collars which are embroidered and they are fastened with fancy filligree buttons of silver or gold. A tight-fitting bodice or corselet made of red or black material is usually worn over the blouse, fastened by laces which are threaded through *snörmärlor* or eyelets of pewter or silver.

The skirts are long and full, usually plain, but occasionally they are brightened by a coloured border or relieved by an apron, the latter being embroidered or woven in coloured stripes, or make of coloured soft leather.

Braid belts knotted at the side with tasselled ends are worn with a square or oval shaped pocket or reticule suspended from

The girl from Blekinge is wearing a square crowned cap and a sleeveless jacket fastened only at the waist

Young girl from Dalarna in her local costume of red, orange and green

From the village of Delsbro, towards the north, the man's costume has an abundance of buttons, the knee bands are of woollen material with red tassels and leather stud decoration. His cap is of knitted wool

An ancient costume from Vanga, still worn by folk dancers. It was originally a farmer's festival attire and consists of full white trousers and footless stockings. The coat is similar to a mediaeval gown of the late fourteenth century

The man's attire from Häverö is formal looking with a top hat, short waistcoat and jacket, and a shirt with a stand-up collar. The light leather breeches and buckled shoes complete the outfit

The headdress from Bara in the southern region of Skäne dates from medieval times. The white kerchief is pinned over a support frame

The man from Dalarna is dressed much like an old-fashioned parson, apart from the buckskin breeches and ornamental garters

them on the left hip. This is usually embroidered in brightly coloured wool.

A shawl, worn like a cape, is fastened in front with a large silver brooch. In the capital city, Stockholm, the shawls were usually in red with a flowered pattern and fringe edged. In Värmland, towards the north, a white shawl, rather like a collar, is edged with a red design, whilst in Ostergotland a similar type of shawl has the front ends tucked into the belt or waistband. In Dalarna, also towards the north, the women wear a white shawl with a red rose design which matches their bonnet made of the same material.

The Swedish headdress is fairly simple. As married women should not show their hair, this is usually covered by a white undercap trimmed with lace, visible at the forehead. Over this is worn a stiff helmet shaped hat with a bow at the back. Young girls may also wear a cap but this, made in two parts, has the join piped in red braid and red ribbons and pompons hanging on the back.

For warmth in winter, short fur-hemmed jackets or cloaks are worn, fastened with a clasp of silver set with red glass.

Mittens, embroidered on the back, and trimmed on the edges with fur, are another interesting feature of their costume.

White knitted stockings worn with black leather shoes or red knitted stockings with coloured and decorated shoes complete the costume.

Shoes, for the most part are short in the toe, with various shaped heels, and may be of coloured leather and decorated with patterns.

As well as wearing functional ornaments such as silver clasps, a considerable amount of purely ornamental jewellery such as earrings, pendants, necklaces and fancy belts are worn.

In earlier times a bride might well have been described as a walking jeweller's shop for on the occasion of her marriage she adorned herself not only with her own jewellery but also with a quantity of borrowed items.

The somewhat clerical looking costume worn by farmers for Sunday best and ceremonial wear was also worn by the bridegroom.

Men's costume, similar to the other Scandinavian countries consists of dark coloured breeches fastened below the knees with red braid and pompons.

The waistcoats, in red or green, fasten down the front with metal buttons. They are cut high at the back to reveal at the

Headdress from Dalarna. The side view shows how it fastens under the chin

The girl from Leksand is wearing a patterened kerchief and neckerchief, and a vertical striped apron over a plain skirt

A headdress from Blekinge, an area known as the Garden of Sweden, shows the folded square tied in such a way as to conceal the hair

In the background can be seen a bell tower of wooden construction. The man on the left is wearing chamois leather breeches with red pompons hanging from the bands over his stockings, and the girl, also from Dalarna, wears a striped apron. The fiddler is from Helsingland and the little girl in the foreground from Dalarna

waist the full long sleeved white shirt worn beneath.

Typical headwear consists of a skull cap in red, blue or black, decorated with red, yellow or blue braid. Other types include top hats or woollen Phyrgian type caps. White or blue hose are worn with black shoes with brass or silver buckles.

Near the east coast in the Halsingland region knitted garments are common for both men and women.

Dark skirts with red appliqué are worn by the women, with blue aprons with a lighter blue and white stripe and a broad red and white band with two red tassels. The red finely striped sleeveless bodice is fastened with hooks, and the knitted jacket, fastened at the side, gives a square neckline. The knitting is designed mainly in red and black, with a fleck of green and white. Red knitted stockings are also worn.

A belt of silver-gilt plates sewn to a sash usually of bright red fabric, and fastened with an open-work silver clasp, was one of the most valued of the women's possessions.

The men wear shirts with high standing collars with a silk scarf around the neck and either a blue jacket with silver buttons or a brightly coloured knitted jacket.

Their breeches could be of a light leather or of blue cloth and were worn with blue stockings. Their caps, made in sections, are bound with black at the seams.

Dalarna, also known as the Land of the Dales, retained the general wearing of traditional folk costume the longest. They have a variety of styles depending on the season and occasion. For instance the basic costume in Leksand consists of a black pleated skirt, a laced bodice and a neckerchief so pinned as to leave two points in the front. The jacket for the summer is in a cloth material, whilst for winter, suede would be worn. Red piping was a popular form of decoration and could be seen on the dark jackets and coats. Characteristic of the dress is the soft leather apron with the bib part elaborately decorated, and the short jacket fringed with thick wool around the neck, hem and cuffs. The colour of the apron depended upon the occasion, brightly striped for everyday wear, and reds, greens or blues for special festivals, whilst dark colours were more appropriate for mourning. The designs of the embroidery denote the area of origin, varying even from parish to parish. Headwear consists of a bonnet or hood-shaped cap.

Peasant girls in early traditional style costume with soft leather aprons, the bib fronts decorated. The jackets are fringed with a thick wool

Red pompons were attached to shoe ties, worn on knee breeches as well as topping various headdresses.

White bonnets are the most typical type of headdress and these are often embellished with ribbons streaming to below the shoulders, but pointed caps in a variety of colours were also worn.

Headdress from the southern province of Blekinge. The shawl is tucked into the bodice

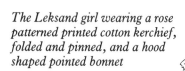

The Leksand girl wearing a rose patterned printed cotton kerchief, folded and pinned, and a hood shaped pointed bonnet

A nineteenth-century costume from Scania, Järnestad. The short jacket fastens with a row of brass buttons, like the waistcoat beneath. The shirt collar is of the stand-up variety, and the breeches of a light leather

The girls from Leksand are wearing white headdresses. Over the plain dark shirts and striped aprons, they are wearing cotton jackets

A typical outfit from the Värmland province

In Södermanland, just south of Stockholm, the festival dress comprises a large square starched cloth folded diagonally with the long ends tied around the head. The skirt hangs from just below the shoulders from a tiny yoke. The bodice and apron hang in folds, trapped at the waist by a wide leather belt

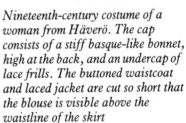

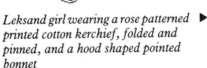

Nineteenth-century costume of a woman from Häverö. The cap consists of a stiff basque-like bonnet, high at the back, and an undercap of lace frills. The buttoned waistcoat and laced jacket are cut so short that the blouse is visible above the waistline of the skirt

Leksand girl wearing a rose patterned printed cotton kerchief, folded and pinned, and a hood shaped pointed bonnet ▶

Both the girl and the small child are wearing Dutch style bonnets. Over the laced bodice the girl is wearing a short jacket, and hanging down from the belt is a reticule. The stockings are knitted

A flat coiled headdress and heavy breast-plate brooches are worn in Scania. The cloth waist belt is decorated with metal plates with the two long ends hanging down to knee length. The blouse has a stand-up collar

The little boy from Rättvik is dressed in a farmer's costume dating from the early twentieth century

A girl from Rättvik wearing a folk costume

Small boy from Rättvik dressed as a farmer. The bands around the base of his breeches have a pompon decoration

Yeoman farmer from Rättvik in an early twentieth century outfit

In Rättvik, another area of the same region, although decoration is similar, the dress is nevertheless different. The skirts are usually dark or bright blue with green edging, and over the bodice a black jacket trimmed with red is worn. The printed neckerchief is folded and pinned to give a narrower effect than in Leksand. The apron, with bold horizontal stripes of red, green, yellow and white forms an integral part of the skirt.

The headdress consists of a square of starched cloth folded diagonally, the point standing out stiffly behind.

A dress worn for festive occasions is made more in the fashion of the Russian *sarafan* – the skirt being attached to a narrow yoke, hanging from just below shoulder level over which is worn a sleeved but short jacket that barely covers the yoke. The apron, gathered at the waist, has a narrow bib.

The headband has an array of streamers, mainly of red ribbon.

For the men, the tradition was to wear full sleeved white shirts beneath dark coloured waistcoats with coloured braid edging, soft leather breeches, and knitted woollen hose with garters from which hung small red woollen pompons.

Men's jackets for festive occasions were long and without collars, usually in white fabric. In eastern Sweden a popular dress at local festivals consists of a long blue coat with a red lining often with a yellow and white horizontal design, knee breeches fastened with a red band and matching tassels and square toed shoes with flap or buckles. A tasselled blue cap completes the outfit.

The young girl from Leksand is wearing a small embroidered cap tied under her chin

Hood shaped pointed cap, almost like ▶ *a phrygian cap from Rättvik, worn by a single girl*

The woman from Rättvik wears an apron of bold horizontal stripes. The back of the skirt is in a plain colour. The pointed headdress is piped at the seams, ending in ribbons and pompons with a white cap beneath

FINLAND

Finland, one of the most northerly countries in the world with a third of its land north of the Arctic Circle, lies in north eastern Europe. It is bounded on the west by the Gulf of Bothnia and Sweden, Norway on the north and west, and on the east by the Soviet Union. To the south lies the Gulf of Finland. The deeply indented coastline is fringed with small islands.

A low lying land, which the Finns call Suomi, meaning swamp land, it consists mainly of lakes and forest areas. Fishing is an important industry as well as agriculture and dairy farming. The summers are short and hot, whilst the winters are cold and the land is snow covered. The Finns, originally nomads, are akin to the Estonians and Magyars and possibly belong to the Mongolian race.

Until 1917 when Finland became independent it had been ruled by Denmark, Sweden and Russia, and the costumes reflect these influences. They are simple but effective. The most popular colours are yellow, blues, reds, greens and white, echoing the summer atmosphere of sun, flowers, forests and the blue lakes. Red, however, is the dominant colour. The geometrical designs are often embroidered in red cross stitch on a white or cream fabric.

The women's costumes are simpler than those in the remainder of Scandinavia. The basic styles consist of a full-sleeved white fine linen blouse with a high neckline edged with a frill or small collar, a sleeveless bodice similar to a waistcoat, laced or fastened with one or two rows of silver buttons, and possibly an apron which either matches the skirt or is of a patterned fabric. It is usual to have a pocket or reticule hanging from a belt at the waist. These were embroidered in various designs depending on the district.

The long woollen skirts often had geometrical or vertical striped designs skirts and white or plain coloured aprons were more popular than towards the east where the more colourful Russian influence was more pronounced.

Old Finnish dress. The girl is wearing a säppali *decorated with metal*

Young peasant girl gathering twigs

30

Finnish Karelian girl wearing a kind of top hat, seen mainly towards the west of the area

Variations in the costume is seen mainly in the shape of the collars, the type of jewellery worn as well as in the headwear. Embroidered kerchiefs are now more popular than the bonnets or caps worn previously.

Headdress consists of small lace-edged caps with a bow at the back, in some regions the ends being long. The bride's headdress at one time was very elaborate and could reach as high as 50 cm. To denote that she is married, a woman usually leaves the top two buttons of the bodice open. A lace edged bonnet also indicates the married status, young girls and children usually wear a headband with ribbon streamers.

Coloured or white stockings were worn with silver buckled shoes in common with the remainder of Scandinavia.

Men's costume was originally a Saxon-like tunic worn with a decorative belt from which hung weapons and other useful articles. Men's costume today consists of a full-sleeved embroidered white shirt with a stand-up collar fastened at the neck with a silver brooch, a colourful striped, double-breasted, waistcoat fastened with two rows of silver or brass buttons, and black or dark blue trousers or breeches matching the jacket, often braided around the edges, and with a stand-up collar fastening with a single button at the top. A brass ornamented belt and a skull cap or brimmed felt hat completes the outfit. In the more northern parts of Finland the men tend to wear moccasin styles shoes like those worn in the summer by the Lapps.

Karelian culture retains vestiges of pre-historic times, the Middle Ages and the Renaissance, and of the days when the western trade routes led from the Gulf of Finland up through Karelia to Ladoga and from there further east. Karelia, as part of the Baltic, was among the areas frequented by Hanseatic merchants. Traces of Finland's eventful history and the isolation of Old Finland from the remainder of the country are seen Karelain folklore, customs and dress.

The costume, influenced by Russian styles, is basically a *sarakko*, which is in the style of a *sarafan*, made of dark or red homespun wool with a coloured border. The decorative front panel has a fastening to the side. In the early nineteenth century blue became a popular colour. The Renaissance custom of embroidering the pleats at the neck of the *sarafan* was retained by the Karelians.

A decorative belt hung with brass pendants and a reticule was hand-made and handed down from mother to daughter.

Karelian man in winter dress. His coat is made of sheepskin leather with a girdle around the waist and high fur boots. The fur cap has the earflaps down for extra warmth

Man's coat in natural coloured thick woollen twill. Gussets are set in the sides to give extra fullness

Two peasants enjoying their leisure. They are playing the kyykka game. They are wearing fur caps, and over his tunic the man sitting astride his friend, is wearing a sleeveless waistcoat. Both are wearing high practical boots

Two singers sitting opposite each other, dressed in loose coats and high boots

A couple enjoying a social dance. The girl is wearing a bodice fastened at the top and waist, a plain dark skirt and a horizontally striped apron. The man's waistcoat is fastened by a double row of buttons and his breeches are tucked into his boots

PLATE 1 NORWAY   The couple on the left are from Voss. The
costume is essentially the same as that of Hardanger. The beaded
plastron is in a geometrical design. The white full-sleeved blouse has
two brooches at the neckline. The white apron has a typical
Hardanger work border.
The man is wearing a popular Scandinavian style outfit. The breeches
fasten below the knees with coloured braid and pompons. White
knitted stockings and buckled shoes show the influence of the eighteenth
century.
The woman on the right is in a ceremonial dress. Her crown is
embellished with filigree work, semi-precious stones and small pendants.
The broad streamers hanging from it are embroidered. She is wearing
dark coloured stockings and low black buckled shoes

PLATE 2 SWEDEN   *The peasant on the* left *is wearing an apron, extremely hard-wearing, made of a soft leather. The bib is elaborately decorated. The short jacket is fringed with a thick wool. The headscarf has a colourful fringing as well. The man in the* centre, *from the Stockholm area, is wearing a sleeveless waistcoat in a striped material over a white full sleeved shirt with a high standing collar. The breeches are fastened at the sides with buttons and end with red braid and pompons. The shoes fasten with buckles. Many of the regional costumes are based on this fashion.*

The girl on the right, *from Ráttvik, is wearing the usual dark blue skirt with a green band at the hem. A horizontally striped apron is worn with a reticule hanging to one side. The pointed headdress is piped along the join in front with red ribbons and pompons hanging behind*

PLATE 3 FINLAND   Both girls are wearing embroidered kerchiefs on their heads. The girl on the left from the south-west area, is wearing a full-sleeved blouse with a sun design brooch at the neckline.
The girl in the centre is wearing an apron in bright colours and a tight fitting bodice.
The costume worn by the man on the right is influenced by the Swedish fashion. His skull cap is decorated with narrow bands of braid. The colourful waistcoat is fastened with metal buttons, and the breeches fasten below the knees with buttons and ribbon decoration. The stand-up collar of the full-sleeved shirt is fastened at the neck with a brooch. White or red stockings are usual with the buckled black shoes

PLATE 4 LAPLAND   *The girl comes from the area between Troms and Finmark in Norway. She is wearing a* kolte *with bands of embroidery and a soft bonnet.*
The Swedish Lapp on the left is wearing a hat with a large red pompon on top and a kolte *fastened with two round brooches.*
The baby's cot in the foreground is made of reindeer skin with a coloured cloth covering tied on with coloured bands.
The little boy, as well as the man in the background, is wearing a cap of the four winds. The tent is made of twigs and animal skins

PLATE 5 LAPLAND   *The man in the* background *is a highlander wearing a cap of the four winds profusely decorated with coloured braid, as is the* kolte. *From his belt hangs a* pukko. *Over his narrow trousers he is wearing high reindeer skin boots.*
The little girl is wearing a blue cloth dress with colourful braid band ornamentation. Her shawl is fringed. Her bonnet, also decorated with braid has ear flaps to protect her from the cold.
The girl on the right *is wearing a fur coat decorated with braid, and a bonnet with a full, soft crown and earflaps. Her mittens are knitted in a typical Lapp design. She is also carrying a* pukko *from her belt.*
Both she and the little girl are wearing woollen socks and moccasins

PLATE 6 DENMARK   On the left is an elaborate costume from
Falster. The darker colours are usually worn by married women. The
large bonnet is made of starched cotton edged with lace and fastened to
a half-bonnet at the back with a ribbon bow. The short sleeved bodice
has bands of embroidered silk from which protrude the long undersleeves
gathered at the wrists. The scarf is tied around her neck with a large
bow in front.
The girl on the right is wearing a country style from Odense. Over her
woollen blouse she is wearing a sleeveless bodice with gold braid edging
and a small gold embroidered design. She is wearing a tight fitting
under-bonnet with the sides down and tied under her chin. The red
half-bonnet worn over this is edged with braid and is also tied beneath
the chin. The girl in the centre, from Fanó, is wearing headwear with
a mask attached. This covers the lower half of the face and acts as
protection against the wind and sand

PLATE 7 ICELAND   Both girls are wearing white blouses beneath their bodices that are laced with gold cord. The girl on the left is in a sleeveless bodice and plain blue apron, more of an everyday costume. Her velvet skull cap has a long tassel with the first 5-6 cm bound with gold rings.
The girl on the right is wearing a more festive dress with an unusual and old style headdress. The bunch of keys hanging from her gold-linked chain belt indicate that she is married.
The man in the centre is wearing breeches fastened below the knees with red cord and tassels. The only decoration on the waistcoat and jacket are the many metal buttons. His woollen cap is worn as protection against the cold

PLATE 8 GREENLAND   The Eskimo baby spends much of his time in the hood of his mother's outer garment. Both men and women wear similar clothes, consisting of jackets and trousers, mainly of bear or seal skin decorated with eider duck or embroidered leather.
The man in the background is in a plain all-fur outfit.
The small child is wearing clothes similar to an adult's, with decorated seal skin boots.
The woman on the right is wearing a fur lined jacket with a brightly beaded collar extending over her shoulders and upper arms, like a cape. The neck, cuffs and trouser bands are of black seal skin

Karelian woman of the nineteenth century. Over her sarakko she is wearing a coat. Her headdress consists of a white veil

Back view of a Karelian woman

Playing the kyykka *game, similar to ninepins, the winner sitting astride the loser who is called the 'giver of the back'*

The headdress and sarakko of this girl from the north Karelia is made of patterned calico, with the apron tied under the armpits

A Finnish Karelian woman. Her hair is hidden beneath the white kerchief. The sleeveless bodice is fastened at the waist with a small clasp and a large brooch at the top

In the southern part of Karelia the women's costumes were heavily embroidered with beads and shells, but towards the north ornamental bands of embroidery with coloured thread or gold brocade ribbons were more popular.

The aprons were the most decorative part of the costumes, being profusely embroidered. For summer they were made of linen with a self material fringe at the hem. For winter they were usually of red wool with gold brocade bands and embroidery. A silk fringe could be added at the bottom.

Around the Gulf of Finland, an early costume, still worn by the older generations, consists of a striped or check skirt with shoulder straps and an embroidered blouse and an apron.

In the western parts of Karelia much of the women's attire was made of black woollen material with white ornamentation, with a band of dark blue lace and drawn-thread trimming around the hem. Bodices matching the skirts were made like short jackets with red braid around the edges.

The women went barefoot in summer but protected the calves of their legs and ankles with tight linen leggings. Moccasins were worn in winter, made of two pieces of leather held together at the ankles with leather thonging.

Young unmarried girls could leave their hair to hang loosely under a stiff headdress studded with beads and edged with lace. When married, the hair was worn up, tied with a red band or *säppäli*, or with a *sykero* made of twigs or tree roots held in place with coloured ribbons, the shape varying in different districts.

Headdresses usually consisted of just a white veil except in inclement weather when a square of striped woollen fabric was worn.

During the nineteenth century the size of the veils developed in various ways. In the south they became so small that the bride's hair had to be cut short in order to be covered by it. Eventually the veil became so tiny that it was just a token worn on the forehead, attached to a little piece of hair.

This costume comes from the west of Finland. The bodice is of a popular design, the top two buttons are left undone, denoting marital status, as does the lace-edged bonnet

Chemise, a combination of bodice and skirt, made in a different materials. The embroidery, of Persian influence, is of coloured wool thread

A woman dressed in nineteenth-century costume from central Finland. The dress is made of various striped materials sewn together ▶

A married woman wearing a pleated white cap with ends hanging behind. On her feet she is wearing moccasins tied on with thonging

The sleeveless bodice is fastened at the waist with a clasp. The blouse with the high necked frill is decorated with a large brooch and a loose bag is fastened to the waist

The Finnish lady is wearing a white cap and a fringed shawl

Woman in a simple national costume

The married woman is wearing a white kerchief entirely hiding her hair, and a large silver brooch on her blouse. The long skirt has geometrical designs and the apron is in narrow stripes

This costume is an older style from
Kaukola. The moccasin type shoes
are similar to those worn by the
Lapps. The large black hat is made
of felt

◄ A typical peasant of the early
twentieth century

A man from central Finland in a
nineteenth century outfit of a striped
jacket and dark breeches and leather
boots

The Karelian girl is wearing a typical
costume and has a band around her
head

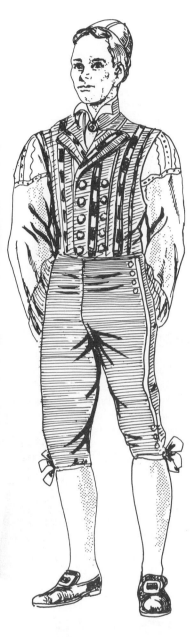

Men generally wore long trousers which were made of two pieces of material without any gusset. They fastened with braided strings, bound at the ankles. Over these was worn a *kaftan*, made of coarse homespun wool, and a loose coat, rather like a dressing gown, with a wide girdle ending in pompons. Long unlined coarse woollen cloaks could be worn over this outfit for extra warmth. Most of the attire was in a light coloured undyed material with red and blue trimmings.

Their fur caps had flaps that, when down, covered their cheeks and ears. Knitted woollen caps were also worn. Fur boots or hide socks were worn under sandals or *labbas* made from the bark of trees.

Karelian man in a Russian influenced style outfit of loose trousers worn beneath a loose coat crossed over and closed with a girdle. His leather cap has the brim and earflaps turned up

The striped waistcoat is fastened with a double row of metal buttons. The white shirt has a stand-up collar fastened at the neck with a brooch. A skull cap and buckled shoes are common

In the severe cold the Karelian fisherman protects his hands with mittens made of water-resistant pig skin or cow hide. He is wearing a woollen cap with the ends tucked into the broad sash worn around his waist over his coat

LAPLAND

The Lapps live in the extreme north-western part of Europe, Lapland being more an ethnic area than a geographical one. It consists of the most northern parts of Norway, Sweden, Finland, the Kola Peninsula and the north-western area of the Soviet Union. They have their own language and culture. Much of their land is known as Finmark and this reaches north to the Arctic circle. It is the Land of the Midnight Sun in summer, and there are six to eight weeks of winter when it is never light.

In Norway there are sea Lapps, river Lapps and mountain Lapps. In Sweden and Finland they are divided into fisher, mountain and forest Lapps, the two latter categories are nomads whose herds of reindeer supply nearly all their needs and they are said to be the true representatives of their race. Those who live along the coastal areas and in the forests have adopted a more settled way of life and the women are striking in their white or grey woollen dresses, the skirts of which are bordered with scarlet and blue and gathered at the waist with brightly coloured sashes.

A Swedish Lapp woman carrying her baby in a skin cradle slung over her shoulders. Her long coat is decorated down the front, and from her belt hangs an assortment of keys, scissors and a reticule

The nomads' dress is practical as well as colourful being suitable for the severest of winters and contrastingly hot summers. The traditional styles have altered very little since the end of the eighteenth century.

Reindeer skins and other furs are used in the making of their clothing including their caps, gloves and footwear, all being richly embroidered. For much of this work they made their own thread by drawing, with their teeth, a metal wire through holes in horn. With a spindle these wires are twisted tightly and evenly around reindeer sinew, giving the thread the appearance of silver. Thread is also spun from hares' fur and used to knit soft and attractive items such as gloves, caps and stockings.

Aged Norwegian Lapp woman wearing a balaclava type floppy bonnet and a plaid shawl

In winter both men and women wear woollen shirts beneath their blue-skirted tunics, decorated with red braid, and blue trousers which are made from reindeer skin. These, in the cold winter months are worn with the hair inside for extra warmth.

Norwegian Lapp girl wearing a colourful cap of the four winds. Her tunic is equally colourful

Also in the Arctic regions a *poncho* style overgarment made of double reindeer skin, is pulled over the head and shoulders, reaching well below the knees. Around the face opening, long white fur is sewn to give further protection against the inclement weather. The large skin gloves are lined with felt and sometimes with the addition of hay to give further warmth. Their high boots, reaching the thighs, are made of reindeer skin and lined with felt. The soles are specially adapted to enable them to slide more easily over the snow.

The colourful Lapp costume is usually completed with a blue woollen cap with large red pompons on top.

A wide leather belt with silver ornamentation and fastened with a silver clasp, is worn over the tunic. Hanging from the belt are essential parts of equipment such as a knife, a silver bag containing a complete tinder box, silver knives and spoons. The women also carry a reticule with needles, reindeer thread, scissors and thimbles for sewing. The numbers of girdles, belts, buttons and rings denotes the owner's wealth.

In summer the fur tunics and trousers are discarded for their summer style tunics, known as *kolte*, made of dark blue felt with decorative bands of red, green or yellow braid, often embroidered, around the neckline, front edges and seams, the colours denoting the district of origin. The tunics worn by the women are longer and fuller, this being achieved by the insertion of gores just below the waistline. Trousers are cut so that there is no seam in the crotch.

A Lapp wearing a tall conical sectional cap and a fur coat

Woman wearing an oddly shaped bonnet with a high extension on the crown, stiffened with a wooden shaper. This style was popular until the end of the eighteenth century

A Lapp child, sitting on the edge of a sledge, is wrapped up warm with a white shawl over the fur coat

A Norwegian Lapp girl wearing a
soft bonnet with side flaps

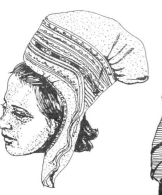

Norwegian Lapp wearing a cap of
the four winds with the points stuffed

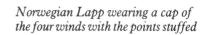

This wedding couple are in festival
attire. The kolte are highly
decorated. The bride is wearing many
round pendants on her shawl, and is
also wearing her wedding rings. The
light coloured moccasins have
pompons at the toes, and the red socks
are worn over the trousers. The bride
is wearing a veil over a cap and the
bridegroom's hat is embellished with
coloured streamers

Both these Swedish Lapps are
wearing caps with pompons on top,
short jerkins and the pukko can be
seen hanging from the belt of the man
on the right

Two Finnish peasant dancers; a
popular past-time after a day's hard
work

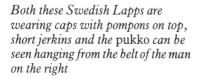

40

Norwegian Lapp kolte with a plain leather belt

The woman is carrying her baby slung over her shoulder in a reindeerskin cradle that can also be suspended from the ceiling at home

A Norwegian Lapp woman wearing a bonnet with flaps to protect her ears

A Norwegian Lapp girl wearing a fur trimmed bonnet. Over her tunic she wears a long apron. The tight trousers are worn with moccasins on her feet

Norwegian Lapp boys wearing peaked caps topped with large pompons

Norwegian Lapp girl standing by the door of her turf hut. They are all dressed in the typical Lapp costume, the child in the foreground showing the back view of a tunic

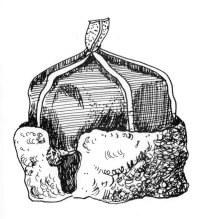

A man's decorated leather cap with the fur lining turned up

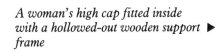

A woman's high cap fitted inside with a hollowed-out wooden support frame ▶

A man's red cloth cap decorated with fur and braid trim with a calico lining

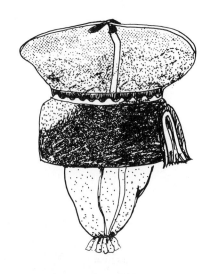

◀ Woman's high cap with an appliquéd band of printed calico over the forehead

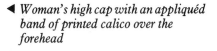

Norwegian Lapp herder wearing a cap of the four winds, and carrying some rope

A Swedish Lapp girl wearing a bonnet with a decorative braid edging. She is also wearing moccasins with turned-up toes

A child wearing a hat of the four winds with just the points left undercorated

The Swedish Lapp woman is wearing a bonnet that covers her ears, and over her fur tunic she has a woollen shawl for extra warmth. The cloth belt is decorated with patterned braid

A Lapp child in the traditional clothing with a tall hat of the four winds. The entire hat is decorated with coloured braid, whilst the four points are in blue with just an edging. He is wearing leather skin coat, the seams of which are decorated with more braid

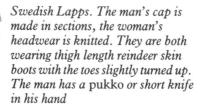

Swedish Lapp wearing a peaked cap topped with pompons. The jacket as well as the cap is decorated with coloured braid

Swedish Lapps. The man's cap is made in sections, the woman's headwear is knitted. They are both wearing thigh length reindeer skin boots with the toes slightly turned up. The man has a pukko or short knife in his hand

The Lapp girl is carrying a cradle made of skin. The baby is tied in with braid bands

Small Finish Lapp boy dressed similarly to an adult

One of the characteristics of Lapp costume is the distinctive headwear. Although different regions have their own variations, basically the design is the same. The men's caps, usually blue, are made in six sections, concical or with the crown square shaped and flat with red tassel hanging from the four corners.

The *cap of the four winds* is an early form of headwear, seldom seen nowadays. It is so called because of its four long points which are stuffed with reindeer hair. The headband has a knot of coloured ribbons hanging to one side. Unmarried men wear this style with all the points to the front.

Women usually wear bobbin shaped hats with flat tops or bonnets with flaps to protect the ears and with a high forward pointing extension on the crown which is stiffened with a hollow wooden frame.

For footwear moccasins made of reindeer skin sewn together are worn, and to give a better fit, as well as warmth, dry grass is often stuffed inside these.

Lapp weddings are among the most colourful in the world. Added to their already bright costumes of scarlet and blue the men have multi-coloured streamers attached to their hats. The bridegroom fastens a small white scarf to his chest with a gold brooch and the bride wears a white veil which is attached to her scarlet bonnet which is tied beneath her chin with a white bow. Often as many as ten large gold brooches are pinned to her silk shawl.

This Swedish Lapp is wearing the early national costume of thick blue cloth and a square crowned cap with four points

Swedish Lapp's cap with large red pompons

A Finnish Lapp herdsman wearing a floppy hat of the four winds, and a blue tunic with red felt trimming around the cuffs, neck opening and shoulders matching the red band around the hat. The high boots are worn over tight trousers

DENMARK

Denmark, the most southerly and smallest of the Scandinavian countries is bounded by Germany to the south, the North Sea lies to the west and on the east it is separated from Sweden by the Öre Sound and the Kattegat; the Skagerrak separating it from Norway in the north.

The country consists of the peninsula of Jutland, and many islands amongst the largest being Zealand, Fünen, Laaland and Bornholm. The Faröe or Sheep Islands lie between Iceland and Norway.

Denmark, being closer than the other Scandinavian countries to the changes in fashion in Europe, the folk costume fell into general disuse sooner, except in a few isolated areas, but there has been a strong revival of such dress in recent years.

Every district and island has its own characteristic variation, especially in the style of headwear, but basically the costumes are all similar, and very practical. Many were cut in the style of the Napoleonic era with high waists, and the jackets, of the spencer type, often with leg-of-mutton sleeves.

Throughout Denmark men's dress differed very little until the beginning of the nineteenth century. In general it consists of a waistcoat and jacket, knee-length breeches, knitted stockings and silver buckled shoes. A top hat or stocking cap completes the outfit. The waistcoat, often of striped homespun material is decorated with silver buttons.

A blue jacket with red braid stripes, fastened up to the neck with matching buttons, is worn with a coloured kerchief tied in a knot. For work the buttons are plain, whilst for special occasions they could be of silver.

The white shirts have stand-up collars around which are worn coloured knotted kerchiefs, red stocking caps with tassels are popular.

In Jutland more lace and white starched cotton was used in the making of the elaborate headwear than in any other area. Small caps were worn towards the back of the head with a frame

The woman from south Jutland is wearing a headscarf tied at the back. The skirt is held up with braces and the cuffs of her bodice are large and ornate

A man from the island of Lyö wearing a long plain coat and striped waistcoat. The woven woollen cap is decorated with braid and a tassel

The old man from the east coast is wearing a homespun woollen tasselled stocking cap

of wide stiffened lace around the face. In other areas such as Aarhus the cap had side wings and was covered with a starched triangular piece of cloth trimmed with white lace.

On the west coast of Jutland at Ringköbing a distinctive style was a large felt top hat worn over a frilled cap.

A medieval type of hood, usually red, was worn by the men, often with a hat on top for formal occasions.

On the island of Laesö between northern Jutland and Sweden the headwear consists of a scarf wrapped around the head in a medieval fashion.

In the Medebo area coloured scarves are tied over the bonnets, whilst on the island of Fanö, in the North Sea off Jutland's west coast, a black mask covering the face, leaving an opening for the eyes, is worn as protection against the swirling sands from the dunes which is whipped up by the strong winds. Similar headwear is also seen on the sandy coastline of Jutland itself. The costumes worn on the island of Fanö are distinctive, although similar styles were also worn on the adjacent islands.

The women's dress consists of a pleated woollen skirt, apron and jacket, all in a dark patterned and matching material.

A headscarf worn over an undercap, the ends tied on the top of the head, and a neckerchief would also be of a similar material, usually a dark red or brown. Blue or purple was worn for mourning.

A bride's headwear consists of a high crown of garlanded flowers. More generally they wear a coloured kerchief which covers the hair entirely, and is tied in such a way that the corners stand out at the sides. For weddings the men wear high crowned hats.

In Odense on the island of Furñen, a red woollen blouse is worn over a sleeveless red bodice which is edged with gold braid, and a cotton apron of checked design is worn over a red skirt. The headdress consists of a tight fitting cotton underbonnet with the sides folded and tied beneath the chin with a small red half-bonnet edged in braid and decorated at the back with a bow worn and also tied under the chin.

On the island of Falster a more elaborate costume can be seen worn by married women. The dark material is brightened by the bodice and cuffs being embellished with bands of mauve embroidered silk sewn to the material and edged with braid. Coloured printed cotton undersleeves, gathered at the wrists, have a frill partially covering the hands. A dark coloured apron with coloured and patterned stripes is worn over a black skirt.

The girl from Äarhus is dressed in a nineteenth century costume. She is wearing a knitted long sleeved underbodice and a tight fitting sleeveless overbodice laced up the front. The headdress consists of a stiff cap with large side fans of stiff lace framing her face

Bridal dress richly embroidered with gold and silver

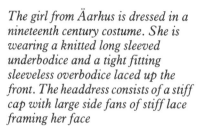

The young girl from the Ringkjöbing area in western Jutland is wearing a top hat over a lace bonnet. She is also wearing a shawl and a plain apron over a horizontally striped skirt

Festival or wedding dress from Rösnos in western Zealand. The silk cap has ribbons hanging behind and fastens under the chin. The skirt is tightly pleated and worn beneath a checked apron

The woman from Skovshoved, near Copenhagen, is in a peasant costume, headscarf and shawl. Wooden clogs similar to the Dutch ones are also worn

The girl from Strömö island is wearing her national costume which is plain and practical. The bodice is laced and the shawl fastened with a brooch in front

This costume from the island of Amager is reminiscent of sixteenth century attire

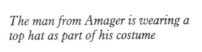

The little girl is dressed in a festive dress with a corsage that is laced, a pinafore and a bonnet. The man comes from north Falster and is dressed in sombre colours. He is wearing the ordinary headwear of a knitted cap, usually in red

The man from Amager is wearing a top hat as part of his costume

From Amager, near Copenhagen, the woman is wearing a bonnet. The large collar is profusely ornamented and the skirt is in fine accordion pleating

A young woman from Fanö wearing a face mask as protection against the wind and sand

This headdress consists of lace, frills and side wings and comes from Salling

A costume from Fünen. The close fitting cap is tied under the chin with a ribbon band. The striped apron covers the entire front of the skirt

The woman from Refsnäs, north west Zealand, is wearing a headscarf and matching neckerchief. Her plain skirt and apron both have a striped border and from her waist hangs a reticule. She is wearing clogs

This country style dress comes from the Odense region, and over the woollen blouse she wears a sleeveless bodice with gold braid edging. A white tight fitting under bonnet with side flaps and fastening under the chin is worn with a small half-bonnet edged in gold and with a bow at the back. This also ties beneath the chin

Young woman from Fanö. This style became extinct in the 1960s. The headscarf was wound tightly over an undercap, the ends knotted on top

A peasant costume from Agger. The bonnet is profusely decorated with ribbons. The apron worn over the striped dress has a cross-over piece around the front

Little girl in festive dress wearing sturdy shoes

This elaborate costume comes from Falster and is worn by married women. The large starched white bonnet is edged with lace with a half-bonnet behind finished with a bow and tied under the chin. The bodice and cuffs have bands on embroidered silk sewn to the garment and are edged with braid. The printed undersleeves are gathered at the wrists and are so long that they partially cover the hands

The man from Refsnäs, north-west Zealand, is wearing a tall black hat, a sleeveless striped waistcoat and breeches

The man is wearing the national costume of Randers

Girl from Fanö wearing a headscarf wound and tied around the head, completely covering her hair. The materials for the dress are of a heavy woollen type needed for warmth in the inclement weather of the area

The girl from the island of Bornholm is wearing a lace bonnet with floral decoration tied under the chin with a ribbon bow. The patterned shawl is tucked in at the waist under the plain apron

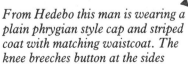

From Hedebo this man is wearing a plain phrygian style cap and striped coat with matching waistcoat. The knee breeches button at the sides

A woman wearing a close fitting cap tied under the chin. She is from the small island of Dreiö

This man comes from east Jutland. He is wearing the typical yellow breeches also seen in Sweden. The striped jacket buttons to the neck around which is worn a small coloured kerchief. He is wearing a stocking woollen cap as worn by most fishermen

53

The large white starched bonnet edged with lace, angled to shade the face, is fastened to a black half-bonnet with a blue ribbon that is tied under the chin.

The Faröes, now a self governing group of islands in the North Atlantic, preserve many old customs. The traditional costume consists of a long dress worn with a shawl over the shoulders, and the men wear smart silver-buttoned suits.

Folk costumes can still be seen as everyday wear by the fisherfolk on some of the islands and in the coastal areas. For weddings and festivals they are also worn on the mainland.

The most popular colours, green, red and yellow, represent the colours of the seasons and landscape.

Very often the bodice and skirts were made of matching material. The many variations include skirts with red stripes on a dark background and a blue bodice, or yellow stripes on a red background with a plain red bodice.

The apron, reaching almost to the hem of the skirt, is often of a checked design in a variety of colours. A white apron decorated with *hedebo* work, the best known style of Danish embroidery is also popular. Some aprons mainly of a cotton material, although of silk for special occasions, are so large that they resemble skirts and in early times were thought to give protection against werewolves.

The headdress usually consists of a simple bonnet of silk or velvet which which can be plain or embroidered. Those worn by married women are usually dark in colour, whilst young girls wear white. Checked shawls or neckerchiefs are worn over the bodices. Red checks on a dark background signify happiness, whilst for mourning blue or green checks on a navy blue background are worn.

Occasionally sleeveless bodices in a constrasting colour are worn over the blouse or dress.

In Mols, on the east of Zealand, a dark blue bodice is worn with long red sleeves, whilst from the Praesto, also in Zealand, a red and green striped bodice edged with green is worn with green threequarter length sleeves.

In Rösmö, a small island west of Jutland just south of Fanö, an apron in a green and yellow checked design on a dark background is worn over a red skirt.

On the main island of Zealand the Dutch influence can be seen in the costumes, especially the women's headdresses which often consist of stiff white kerchiefs or bonnets with side flaps. Dark green skirts are very popular, as are most dark

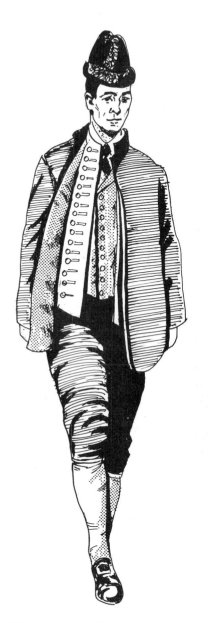

This man from the Faröes, a group of self governing islands in the north Atlantic is wearing a waistcoat and jacket fastened with silver buttons. Knee breeches, knitted socks and silver buckled shoes complete the outfit

54

colours, with ornate embroidery.

On the western side the Rösnös dress depends greatly on the occasion and season. Therefore several costumes are required. Homespun, woven or knitted fabrics are utilised in a variety of ways as well as a selection of coloured ribbons. A dress could consist of a patterned sleeveless bodice worn over a long-sleeved buttoned up underbodice. The knitting is generally in the characteristic self-coloured diamond design.

Pleated skirts with coloured bands are worn with checked aprons. Fine accordion pleating known as cooked pleating, was achieved by putting the damp and carefully pleated skirt, wrapped in a muslin cloth, in a cool bread oven, or by laying freshly baked loaves on it to dampen it before pressing.

Man in typical Faröes costume

A typical costume from the Faroe Islands

These girls are from the island of Strömö, the largest of the Faroe group. The dress is fairly plain, the laced bodice and skirt in the same colour. A traditional fringed shawl and plain apron is also worn

ICELAND

Iceland, situated in the North Atlantic between Norway and Greenland is a roughly oval-shaped island, the coastline being broken by a large number of deep fjords.

The central area, comprised of volcanic rocks, hot springs and glaciers, is uninhabited, the main areas of the small population being along the shores of the fjords where grass is sufficient to support sheep and cattle, and the sea providing a thriving fishing industry. The largest concentration of people is in and around the capital Reykjavik.

The scenery is of great natural beauty, and the climate relatively mild due to the influence of the Gulf Stream.

In contrast to the wide variety of national costume in the other Scandinavian countries, in Iceland there is only one style. The colour is predominately black, possibly because the resources for dyeing are very limited. The folk dress seen nowadays dates from the mid-nineteenth century revival. However, some of the older styles have remained unchanged.

Apart from the general use of *vadmál*, a kind of woollen cloth woven locally, the men are usually dressed in western European fashions. For festive occasions their dress consists of black breeches with a tassel at each knee, a black high neck waistcoat fastened with silver buttons, and a black jacket with matching silver buttons at either side, these being purely decorative. A small scarf is knotted at the neck.

As a protection against the winter elements leather gaiters are worn over stout leather shoes and, for warmth, a woollen skull cap.

The women wear long, full black woollen skirts, often embroidered in silk above the hemline, with a black long-sleeved bodice revealing a narrow white strip of the blouse at the front and a white frill along the neckline. The edges of the bodice are fastened by a large gold or silver filigree brooch. The decoration down either side of the front is usually in gold and green embroidery in the shape of these designs are reminiscent

Icelandic milkmaid. Her everyday dress serves also as a riding habit

56

of their Celtic or Viking background. Younger girls generally wear sleeveless bodices. White or coloured blouses worn beneath the bodices have long full sleeves and the neckline could be high ending in a frilled collar. The belt is of metal links or may be embroidered. A bunch of keys hanging from the belt indicates marital stutus.

The headdress is most unusual. A fine white veil is draped over a small white hat with a curved crown, and kept in position by a gold circlet fitted around the head.

For everyday dress or *peysuföt*, in place of the long-sleeved bodice, a laced corselet is worn over a long-sleeved white blouse, and a light coloured apron, often blue, over the black full skirt. A black velvet or silk scull cap or *húfa* is worn with a long tassel on the right side fixed with gold rings.

Footwear consists of stout leather shoes.

Brides wear a black woollen dress with the neckline and shoulders as well as the sleeves embroidered with oak leaves and vine tendrils in gold and silver threads. The hem of the skirt is similarly decorated. The headwear, covered with a veil, is shaped like a helmet and is ornamented with silver stars. The belts, clasp and buttons are all of gold and silver filigree work.

Festival dress

Festive costume as worn since the 1860s, specially designed. It is black with braid decoration. The bodice is fastened with a brooch and the neckline and cuffs edged with lace and embroidered with gold metalic thread. The tall curved headdress is covered with a white veil with a gilded circlet around the front

Icelandic bridal dress. The headwear is like a helmet from which hangs a white veil. The dress is of silk or velvet with an ermine-trimmed cloak

Icelandic bridal costume

Festival dress. The sleeveless bodice is laced. The white blouse is gathered at the neckline and a gold chain and pendant is worn

58

GREENLAND

Greenland, which belongs to Denmark, is the world's largest island and is noted for its glaciers. It lies north-west of the mainland of North America with Iceland lying some 320 km off its north-east coast.

The few Eskimos that remain live mainly in the most northerly parts of the island along the coast. Their clothes, suited to the severe cold climate, are made of the skins of various animals such as caribou and seal. Both men and women wear seal skin trousers and over these boots or *kamiker* made from skins which are first chewed by the women to soften them.

The dress worn by the men is made entirely of animal skin and fur. It is plain and practical. The jackets often have hoods attached, and sometimes two pairs of trousers are worn to give extra warmth.

The women's fur-lined jacket could be decorated with a brightly coloured beadwork collar, often so large that it covers both the shoulders and upper arms like a cape. The high neck and cuffs could be decorated with black seal skin bands. Blouses, now made mainly of imported fabric, are decorated with lace. Their trousers are ornamented with eider duck feathers and also have bands of black seal skin. The style of hood worn by the women has a 'tail' in which they can carry their baby.

Eskimo woman with her child carried in the hood of her fur jacket

59

*Eskimo hunter in winter costume
wearing sealskin trousers and jacket*

*Eskimo woman wearing a brightly
patterned bead collar extending over
the shoulders and upper arms. The
high neck, cuffs and trouser bands
are of black sealskin, and the leather
sealskin boots are fur lined. She is
with a young Eskimo boy*

An Eskimo woman in her home-
made sealskin garment with
embroidered leather trimming.
Women wear trousers and jackets like
the men. This woman has bead
decoration on her coat

Ornamented skin costume and a ▶
typical Greenland hairstyle

An Eskimo's full fur outfit

Small Eskimos wearing high skin
boots and dressed as their elders

61

GLOSSARY OF COSTUME TERMS

Appliqué	Cut-out ornamental work applied to the surface of another material
Bara	Strip of cloth worn around the head
Bursölje	Belt buckle with six projections
Drawn-thread work	Ornamental openwork achieved by pulling out threads of the fabric and embroidering the edges and openings thus made
Glit	Cross stitch
Hedebo work	The best known style of Danish embroidery which comprises lace-filled stitches worked on white linen, the designs depicting convensionalised bird, animal, floral or human forms
Homespun	Fabric woven at home; loose and rough giving the appearance of tweed
Hufá	Icelandic tasseled cap
Kaftan	Long-sleeved type of coat worn with a sash
Kamiker	Boots made of reindeer skin
Kolte	A blue felt tunic with coloured band decoration worn by Lapps
Krullesaum or *Krotasaum*	Scroll embroidery
Labbas	Sandals made from the bark of trees
Maler	Metal eyelets originally plain rings
Peplum	Short flounce attached to a jacket or coat at the waist
Peysuföt	Everyday dress consisting of jacket and skirt worn in Iceland
Plastron	The ornamental front of the bodice of a woman's dress
Pukko	Short knife
Reticule	Loose pocket hung from a belt

Norwegian Lapp in his popular headwear and kolte *with an ornamental belt*

Rosesaum	Rosework embroidery
Säppali	Headband worn by married women
Sarafan	Skirt and bodice combined, or a skirt with shoulder straps
Sarakko	A *sarafan* style of dress
Skaut	Headdress consisting of a starched triangular embroidered kerchief over a leather foundation
Snörmärlor	Eyelets
Sykero	Headwear made of twigs or tree roots decorated with ribbons, and supporting a veil
Tjeld	A striped shawl
Vadmál	Woollen cloth woven locally in Iceland

The Hardanger skaut *or headdress is of a finely pleated linen and the* plastron *and beadwork belt in a geometric design*

BIBLIOGRAPHY

BRUHN, W, and TILKE, M, *Pictoral History of Costume*, Zwemmer 1955

FOX, L *Folk Costume of Western Europe*, Chatto and Windus 1975

GILBERT, JOHN, *National Costumes of the World*, Hamlyn 1972

HAMMERTON, J A, *Lands and Peoples*, Amalgated Press 1927

HAMMERTON, J A, *Peoples of all Nations*, Amalgated Press 1922-1924

HARROLD, R and LEGG, P, *Folk Costumes of the World*, Blandford Press 1978

HOLME, CHARLES, editor, *Peasant Art in Sweden, Lapland and Iceland*, The Studio 1910

JAMES, ALAN, *Lapps, Reindeer herders of Lapland*, Wayland 1986

KLEIVAN , KARE, *Norge i Nord*, Knut Aune Kunstforlaf A/S

LIDDLE, Rev William and Mrs Liddle, *Peeps at Many Lands – Sweden*, A & C Black 1911

MANN, KATHLEEN, *Peasant Costume in Europe*, A & C Black 1950

PRIMMER, KATHLEEN, *Scandinavian Peasant Costume*, A & C Black 1939

SNOWDEN, J, *Folk Dress of Europe*, Mills and Boon 1979

STEWART, J S, *Folk Arts of Norway*, Constable 1972

TILKE, M, *Folk Costumes from Eastern Europe*, Zwemmer 1978

Customs of the World, Hutchinson 1913

National Geographica magazines

An eyelet or maler

INDEX